A MODERN DAY CINDERELLA STORY

Re-Create Your Crown

RISE ABOVE LIMITING BELIEFS AND RECLAIM YOUR POWER

By De'iona Monay

© 2024 De'iona Monay. All rights reserved.

No part of this publication may be reproduced, distributed, or transmitted in any form by any means, including photocopying, recording, or other electronic or mechanical methods, without the prior written permission of the publisher, except in the case of brief quotations embodied in critical reviews and certain other noncommercial uses permitted by copyright law.

For permission requests, write to the publisher, addressed, "Attention: Permissions Coordinator" at the address below

784 SW 14th st. Moore, OK 73160

ISBN: 979-8-9916749-0-4 (Hardbound)
ISBN: 979-8-9916749-1-1 (eBook)
ISBN: 979-8-9916749-2-8 (Paperback)

Disclaimer: The content of this book is based on the author's personal journey and experiences in overcoming limiting beliefs. She is not a mental-health professional, and the information provided is not intended as a substitute for professional advice, diagnosis, or treatment. Please consult with a licensed mental health professional for any concerns or issues related to your mental well-being.

Front cover image by: Artist
Book design by: Brandy M. Miller

Fonts: Abhaya Libre, Aniyah*
*Aniyah font commercial license purchased for use

First printing edition: 2024

Dedication

This book is dedicated to every girl who has lived a Cinderella story—the ones who were made to feel like they weren't enough, who were told they didn't deserve love, happiness, or success. To the girls who've faced rejection, felt unseen, or struggled to find their voice in a world that tried to dim their light.

May you find the strength to rewrite your story, reclaim your worth, and know that you are deserving of everything you dream of. Your crown has always been yours—now it's time to wear it with pride.

Table of Contents

Dedication	3
Chapter 1: The Seeds of a Cinderella Story	7
Chapter 2: The Father I Never Had	11
Chapter 3: Miracles	17
Chapter 4: The Weight of Limiting Beliefs	21
Chapter 5: The Dark Side of Pretty Girl Privilege	29
Chapter 6: The Art of Personal Development	33
Chapter 7: The Only Way Out Is In	39
Chapter 8: Living in Alignment	45
Chapter 9: The Power of Stillness	49
Chapter 10: The Art of Transformation	55
Chapter 11: The Ripple Effect of Transformation	59
Chapter 12: Embracing the Journey	63
Chapter 13: The Foundation of Faith	69
Chapter 14: The Power of Obedience	73
Chapter 15: The Power of Connections	77
Chapter 16: Forgive Yourself	81
Chapter 17: Re-Create Your Crown	85
Workbook: Re-Create Your Crown (6-Weeks)	89
Acknowledgements	93
About the Author: De'iona Monay	95

Chapter 1: The Seeds of a Cinderella Story

My life began as a complex tapestry woven with the threads of my mother's past—a past marked by rejection and a constant search for belonging and protection. My mother, who was adopted by her stepfather, entered a family that never truly accepted her. She was always the outsider, treated with subtle but unmistakable cruelty that made her feel less-than and unworthy of the love that was so freely given to her siblings. This was the environment I was born into, an atmosphere thick with the echoes of her pain and the unspoken understanding that I too was somehow not enough.

From an early age, I became acutely aware of the stark difference in how we were treated compared to the rest of the family. It wasn't subtle—it was glaringly obvious. While they enjoyed nicer cars and clothes, my mom, sister, and I were left to fend for ourselves, relying on Section 8, food stamps, and WIC. We were often handed down their old clothes in black trash bags—always the oldest, most worn-out things. I can still remember the distinct smell of my grandmother's house whenever I opened those bags. It was a reminder of the divide between us.

My grandparents sent all their children to college, but they neglected to do the same for my mom. I'll never forget the day when my mom and I got into a verbal argument with her siblings. I was 14 at the time, and one of my aunts turned to my mom and said, "And don't call and ask my momma for any more money," as if they didn't share the same mother. It was a real-life Cinderella story. My mother, though the firstborn, was treated like a stepchild after my grandmother remarried. Instead of an evil stepmother, my mom had an evil stepfather. She was forced to take care of her siblings and eventually sent to live with my great-grandmother, who raised her.

But the moment that really opened my eyes came when I was 31 years old. My son was 5, and I had a speaking engagement. I asked my grandmother if she could watch him for a few hours, but she refused. She said she couldn't because she had her "other" grandkids and that my uncle—my mom's younger brother—would be upset. The most painful part was that she didn't see anything wrong with it; she said it without a hint of remorse. That was when I woke up. The favoritism was blatant, and it cut deeply.

See, I realized that this was not just an oversight—it was a clear message that my mother, and by extension, me and my son, were not worthy of the same love or opportunities.

These experiences were not just isolated events; they were part of a larger pattern that left me feeling like an outsider in my own family. I grew up watching my cousins receive the finer things in life, support and opportunities that were denied to me, my siblings, and my mother. The message was clear: we were different, and not in a way that was celebrated or valued. This exclusion sowed the seeds of inadequacy in me, reinforcing the belief that there was something inherently wrong with me, something that made me less deserving of love and acceptance.

Adding to this was the fact that my family placed a high value on education, particularly college degrees. In a family where success was measured by academic achievement, I felt like an outsider once again because I chose a different path. I am an entrepreneur, and while I have found fulfillment in this path, it was often seen as less than by my family and others around me. My decision to forgo the traditional route of college only deepened my feelings of not being good enough. It was another way I felt I did not measure up to the expectations placed upon me.

These early experiences planted the seeds of my limiting beliefs. I began to believe that I was not worthy of the love I craved. Why else would I be treated this way? I did not understand the complexities of my mother's past or the reasons behind her pain—I only knew the effect it had on me. I started to see myself as inadequate, unworthy of affection or kindness, and this belief became the lens through which I viewed the world.

As I grew older, these feelings of inadequacy began to manifest in more profound ways. I became increasingly insecure, questioning everything about myself—my looks, my intelligence, my value as a person. I would stare at myself in the mirror, searching for something that would explain why I felt so unloved, so invisible. The more I searched, the more I found flaws, imperfections that seemed to confirm what I already believed: I wasn't good enough. This was the story I began to write for myself, a story of not being enough, a story of a girl who would never truly be loved.

Call to Action

Most of the beliefs that limit us today have their roots deep in our childhoods, planted long before we even had a say in who we wanted to become. But here's the thing: healing begins at the root. If we never go back and examine where our beliefs came from, we'll continue to carry them like baggage, letting them dictate our lives without even realizing it.

I challenge you to take a brave step today. Start by reflecting on your childhood. What were the messages you received? How were you treated? And how have those early experiences shaped the way you see yourself now? This is where the real work begins—by getting to the root of your trauma, your limiting beliefs, and the story you've been telling yourself for far too long.

Ask yourself: What beliefs about myself did I inherit that I didn't choose? How has my past shaped the way I show up in the world today?

When you begin to pull back the layers and see the roots of your pain, that's when you can start to rewrite your story. That's when you can re-create your crown. Remember, you don't have to remain the same. You have the power to dig deep, to pull out the weeds, and to plant new seeds of worth, love, and abundance. Your childhood may have shaped you, but it doesn't have to define your future. Start today—begin at the root.

Chapter 2: The Father I Never Had

Growing up without a father or a male role model left a void in my life that I didn't know how to fill. That void was like an open wound, silently aching for the love, affection, and protection I never received. I was a young girl, yearning for the kind of unconditional love that I imagined a father would provide. I longed for someone to make me feel safe, valued, and cherished—feelings that were foreign to me in the environment I grew up in.

My father was absent for most of my life. I was the third oldest of 13 children he had with various women, and while I knew him, we never had a relationship. I was just one of many, another child in a long line, and that reality only deepened my sense of being unworthy of love.

When I was 14 years old, I met an older boy. A parent's worst nightmare. He was 19, older, and seemingly wiser. To me, he was everything I thought I needed. He paid attention to me in ways that no one else ever had. He told me I was beautiful, that he cared about me, that he would protect me. Those words, that attention—it was intoxicating to a young girl with an absent father. It was the first time I felt noticed, the first time I believed someone might truly care about me. I didn't see the red flags. How could I? I was young, gullible, and naïve. I was desperate for the affection and validation that I had been starved of my entire life.

Shortly after meeting this boy, my life took a dark and defining turn that solidified those early feelings of unworthiness. He took advantage of my innocence and sexually abused me. This experience shattered any remaining belief that I was valuable. But unlike so many others who suffer in silence, my mother knew. She took me to the doctor and witnessed the doctors face expression as she gave me my womanly examine and discovered that I not only was sexually abused, but my entire life could now be different!

The doctor later told myself and my mother that I had contracted a sexually transmitted disease that I would not be able to get rid of. At that moment, I remember my heart feeling like it had been ripped from my chest. During that moment I realized how serious sex was. It wasn't just something fun to do. It could change everything! My mother was saddened by the news but too deep in her own pain and struggles to provide the emotional support and guidance that I desperately needed.

My mother, who had always been entangled in her own feelings of inadequacy and unworthiness, was there physically, but emotionally, she was absent. She was a woman battling her own demons, and while she did what she could for me, it was not enough to fill the void that the abuse had created. In those moments, I felt utterly alone.

The one person I could have leaned on was too consumed by her own pain to truly be there for me. Adding to this sense of isolation was the departure of my older sister, the only person I felt understood me. She joined the Marines at a crucial point in my life, leaving me to navigate this dark period on my own. Her absence was a profound loss—I had always looked up to her, and with her gone, I felt like I had lost the only ally I had. The loneliness was suffocating, and I began to retreat further into myself, burying my pain beneath layers of silence and shame.

The shame was overwhelming. Despite knowing that what happened to me wasn't my fault, I couldn't shake the feeling that I was somehow to blame. The trauma reinforced everything I had come to believe about myself—that I was only worth what others could take from me, that my value was tied to what I could offer, particularly to men. This belief became the foundation of my identity, shaping how I saw myself and how I interacted with the world.

But the worst part was the silence. Although I had confided in my mother, the emotional support I needed wasn't there, and I felt I couldn't turn to anyone else. How could I speak about something that confirmed everything I feared was true about myself? How could I reveal to others what I believed to be my own deep, inherent flaw? So, I kept quiet, burying the pain deep inside, where it festered and grew, intertwining itself with the already toxic beliefs I held about myself.

The silence was a heavy burden to bear, but it was also a shield. As long as I didn't speak about it, I could pretend that it hadn't happened, that I wasn't as broken as I felt. But the truth was, the silence only deepened my wounds. It isolated me, cutting me off from any possibility of healing or support. I was alone with my thoughts, and those thoughts were anything but kind.

After my abuse, my mother, recognizing my desperate need for a male figure, sent me to live with my father. She hoped that he would guide me, talk to me from a male perspective, and offer the protection I had been missing. But those hopes were quickly dashed.

Unfortunately, my father paid zero attention to me. He was constantly working, leaving me with his mother and girlfriend most of the time. I had so much freedom—too much, in fact. It wasn't a better environment at all. I was still alone, still yearning for the love and guidance that never came.

The living arrangement didn't last long. My father and I ended up getting into a verbal argument around money—an argument that would be our last interaction for years. Shortly after, he left me a voicemail that cut deeper than any other wound. He told me that he never wanted to hear from me again.

I was devastated. Not only did I feel like I wasn't good enough for the men in my life, but now, I wasn't even good enough for my own father.

That voicemail echoed in my mind for years, reinforcing the belief that I was unworthy of love, that I was destined to be abandoned, that I would never be enough. The silence of my suffering grew louder, a constant reminder that I was alone, unwanted, and unlovable.

Call To Action

As I reflect on this Chapter, I'm reminded of how deeply I used to bury my yearning for a father. I would tell myself it didn't bother me and convince myself I didn't need him. I watched others wait for their fathers, but I wasn't that girl—I buried it deep. I told myself I didn't care. Even into adulthood, I clung to the narrative that I turned out fine without him, that I was strong enough to be okay on my own.

But here's the truth: the absence of a father leaves an imprint on your heart and mind, whether you acknowledge it or not. It shows up in ways you don't expect. It affects your relationships, the way you see yourself, and how you show up in the world. You might tell yourself that you're fine, but somewhere beneath that surface, there's a wound that hasn't healed.

I challenge you today to stop and reflect. Ask yourself: How has my relationship, or lack of relationship, with my father impacted my life? How have I buried that pain, and where does it show up in my actions, my decisions, and my beliefs about myself?

It's time to dig deeper. It's time to stop pretending that the pain doesn't exist. Because only when we confront it, only when we acknowledge how it has shaped us, can we begin to heal. You are worthy of love, protection, and belonging—whether you received it from your father or not. But healing starts by facing the truth. Start today, go to the root of your pain, and allow yourself the space to heal."

Chapter 3: Miracles

In the midst of this darkness, something miraculous happened—something that would change the course of my life and strengthen my relationship with myself, and God forever.

About a year after this nightmare began, my mother decided to move us to a new city. She recognized that we both needed a fresh start, a new beginning where we could leave behind the pain of the past and create a new future. In this new city, my mother made it a priority to get us involved in church. For the first time, I began to build a personal relationship with God. The church became a place of refuge, a place where I could begin to heal the wounds that had been inflicted on my heart and soul.

As I spent more time in church, as I began to pray and seek God's guidance, something inside me started to change. I started to feel a sense of hope, a sense that, just maybe, I could be free from the pain that had been consuming me. I did not know how or when, but I began to believe that God could heal me, that He could take away the hurt and give me a new beginning.

And then, the miracle happened.

One day, we received a phone call from the doctor. The doctor's voice on the other end of the line was filled with disbelief and amazement. She said, "It's a miracle, we ran the test multiple times and see no sign of the disease." My test results had come back negative. The disease was gone. It was as if it had never been there.

In that moment, I knew that something greater was at work in my life. I knew there was a God and that God had intervened in my life. He had given me a second chance. It was a moment of pure joy, a moment of celebration, a moment that marked the beginning of my walk with God.

This miracle was a turning point in my life. It was the moment when I realized the power of God and that I meant something to him. God revealed to me at an early age that I was not bound by the mistakes or the pain that had been inflicted upon me. It was the moment when I began to see myself not as a victim, but as a survivor, as someone who had been given a new lease on life.

The silence of suffering had been broken, and in its place was a new song—a song of hope, healing, and redemption. I realized that I was just a child, a young girl who did not know any better, who was trying to fill a void that no one had ever told her she could fill herself.

However, this was just the beginning of my journey. The abusive relationship became my first real definition of love. It became the lens through which I viewed all future relationships. It taught me that love was something painful, something that required sacrifice and suffering. It taught me that love was about control, about pleasing someone else at the expense of myself.

In the years that followed, the abuse became a defining feature of my identity emotionally. I began to believe that I was only worth what others could take from me, that my value lay solely in what I could offer to others. This belief became the foundation for the decisions I would make in the years to come.

Call To Action

As I reflect on the miracle that changed my life, I'm reminded of the incredible power of God's love. In my darkest moments, when I believed I wasn't enough, when I thought my pain would define me, God stepped in. He healed my body and my spirit. But it wasn't just about the physical healing—it was about God showing me that His love is greater than any pain, greater than any trauma, and greater than any definition of love I had ever known.

I was also told I might not be able to have kids because I had the disease for so long. But here I am, with a healthy 9-year-old son—my miracle baby—who shares the same birthday as me. God gave me the greatest gift on my born day, and every time I look at him, I'm reminded that miracles are real.

Now, I ask you—what was your first real definition of love? Was it from your father, your mother, or perhaps your first relationship? What was that early memory of love, or maybe even the lack of it, that still replays in your mind? Take a moment to reflect on how that definition of love has shaped the way you see yourself and the way you show up in your relationships.

And here's the beautiful part—no matter what your first experience of love was, no matter how broken or painful it may have been, God's love is something entirely different. God's love is not conditional, it's not based on what you can give or how much you've suffered. God's love is healing, it's unconditional, it's freeing, and it's powerful beyond measure. Just as God healed my body, He can heal your heart, your spirit, and your soul.

So, I challenge you to open your heart to the possibility of God's love. What would your life look like if you fully accepted the love that God has for you, a love that asks for nothing in return but gives you everything? That's the power of God's love—it's transformative, it's redemptive, and it's available to you right now." So, go get it!

Chapter 4: The Weight of Limiting Beliefs

As I transitioned into adulthood, the beliefs that had taken root in my childhood began to manifest in more tangible ways. The seeds planted by the experiences of my youth—feeling like an outsider in my own family, being denied the same opportunities as others, and enduring the trauma of sexual abuse—had grown into a full-blown narrative that dictated my every decision.

One of the most significant areas where these limiting beliefs showed up was in my romantic relationships. I had internalized the idea that my worth was tied to how others perceived me, particularly men. I was desperate to be chosen, to be loved, and I believed that to secure that love, I had to prove myself worthy. But what did worthiness look like to me at that time? It wasn't about who I was as a person—my character, my kindness, my intelligence. No, it was about what I could offer to others, particularly in terms of physical and emotional availability.

I started to see myself through the lens of how others treated me. If a man didn't choose me, I felt it was because I wasn't good enough. If he did choose me, I believed

I had to go above and beyond to keep his attention and affection. I would overextend myself, giving everything I had to prove my worth, even if it meant compromising my own values and well-being. I would lose myself in the process, molding myself into what I thought others wanted, rather than standing firm in who I truly was.

This behavior was rooted in a belief that I was only worth what I could give, and that if I were not constantly giving, I would be discarded. This belief was reinforced by the men in my life who treated me as though my only value lay in what I could offer them physically. I internalized their words and actions, allowing them to dictate how I saw myself. If they saw me as only good for one thing, then that must be all I was good for, right?

But this belief was not just about how others treated me—it was also tied to my own deep-seated fears and insecurities. I was terrified of not being chosen and being seen as less than. I had spent my entire life feeling like I wasn't good enough, and I was desperate to prove that narrative wrong. But in my desperation, I did not realize that I was reinforcing that very narrative. By bending over backwards to please others, I was telling myself that I was not worthy of love or attention unless I was constantly proving my worth.

For years, I constantly felt the need to overcompensate, to go the extra mile, to prove that I was worth something. But no matter how much I gave, it never felt like enough. The more I gave, the emptier I felt, because I was giving from a place of fear and insecurity, rather than from a place of genuine self-worth.

This cycle of giving and feeling empty became a vicious cycle that was difficult to break. The more I gave, the more I lost myself, and the more I lost myself, the more I felt the need to give to fill the void. It was a never-ending cycle of self-sacrifice that left me feeling depleted and unfulfilled. But at the time, I did not see a way out. I did not know how to break free from the chains of my limiting beliefs. All I knew was that I was tired—tired of giving, tired of proving, tired of feeling like I was never enough.

Furthermore, the need to prove myself extended beyond just romantic relationships. It seeped into every aspect of my life, from my career to my friendships to my interactions with strangers. As an entrepreneur, I was driven by a desire to create something of my own, to build a business that reflected my values and passions. But despite my ambitions, I often found myself hitting an invisible ceiling when it came to making more money and achieving the level of success, I knew I was capable of.

This ceiling was not made of glass; it was made of the deeply ingrained beliefs I held about my worth. These beliefs were so deeply embedded in my psyche that I was not even fully aware of them. I did not consciously think, "I'm not worthy of making more money." But my actions, decisions, and the way I approached my work were all subtly influenced by this underlying belief. It was as if I was carrying around an invisible weight, one that held me back from fully stepping into my potential and claiming the financial rewards that were within my reach.

One of the ways this limiting belief manifested was in how I priced my services. As an entrepreneur, setting prices is a crucial aspect of running a successful business.

But I often found myself undercharging for my work, convinced that if I charged more, people would not see the value in what I was offering. I was afraid that if I asked for what I was worth, clients would turn away, leaving me with nothing. This fear was not just about losing clients—it was about the deeper fear of being seen as unworthy and being rejected for daring to claim my true value.

This belief also showed up in how I negotiated contracts and deals. I would often settle for less than what I deserved, afraid to ask for more, worried that I would be seen as greedy or demanding. I did not believe I was in a position to ask for higher rates, better terms, or more favorable conditions, even when I knew I had the skills and experience to back it up. I convinced myself that I should be grateful for what I was getting, even if it was not enough to truly sustain me or my business.

But the truth was, this wasn't just about being practical or cautious—it was about the limiting belief that I wasn't worthy of more. This belief was like an invisible script running in the background, dictating my actions without me even realizing it. I would tell myself that I was being realistic, that I couldn't ask for more because the market wouldn't support it, or because others in my industry weren't charging that much. But deep down, the real reason was that I didn't believe I deserved more. I didn't see myself as someone who could command higher rates, who could stand firm in their value and expect to be compensated accordingly.

This belief wasn't just about money—it was about worthiness. It was about the stories I had internalized over the years, the messages that told me I wasn't enough, that I had to work harder, give more, and settle for less because that was all I deserved. These stories were reinforced by the experiences of my childhood, by the feeling of being an outsider, by the trauma of being treated as less-than by my own family. They were reinforced by the relationships where I overextended myself, by the men who treated me as though my only value lay in what I could offer them physically.

But the most insidious thing about these beliefs was that I wasn't fully aware of them. They operated beneath the surface, shaping my actions and decisions in ways I didn't recognize. I was afraid to step into my full potential, to claim the success and financial abundance that was rightfully mine, because I didn't believe I deserved it.

This limiting belief created a cycle of self-sabotage that kept me stuck. I would set goals for myself, only to fall short because I didn't fully believe I could achieve them. I would work hard, put in the effort, but when it came time to reap the rewards, I would find a way to undermine myself, to keep myself small. I would make excuses, procrastinate, or settle for less, all because I was afraid of what it would mean to truly step into my power and claim the success that was mine for the taking.

But the irony was that no matter how much I undercharged, no matter how much I settled for less, it never made me feel more secure or validated. It only reinforced the belief that I wasn't enough, that I had to keep proving myself, keep giving more and more in order to be worthy of success. The more I gave, the more I depleted myself, and the more I depleted myself, the more I felt like I had to give.

This cycle left me exhausted, unfulfilled, and constantly chasing a sense of worthiness that I could never quite grasp.

Breaking free from this cycle required me to confront these limiting beliefs head-on. It required me to go inward and examine the stories I had been telling myself for so long, to challenge the narrative that I wasn't enough, that I didn't deserve to make more money or achieve the success I dreamed of. It required me to rewrite those stories, to replace the belief in my unworthiness with a belief in my inherent value and deservingness.

This wasn't an easy process. It required me to step outside of my comfort zone, to start charging what I was truly worth, to set boundaries and stand firm in them, even when it was uncomfortable. It required me to trust that I could make more money without sacrificing my values or my well-being, that I could achieve success without having to constantly prove myself or overextend myself. It required me to believe, genuinely believe, that I was worthy of success, of financial abundance, of everything I had ever dreamed of.

As I began to shift these beliefs, I started to see changes in my career and my finances. I began to attract clients who were willing to pay what I was worth, who valued my work and respected my boundaries. I started to see opportunities for growth and expansion that I had never noticed before, because I was no longer blinded by my fear of unworthiness. I started to make more money, not because I was working harder or giving more, but because I was finally operating from a place of self-worth and abundance.

This journey wasn't just about making more money—it was about reclaiming my power, about stepping into my full potential and realizing that I was capable of so much more than I had ever allowed myself to believe. It was about breaking free from the chains of my limiting beliefs and embracing the truth of who I was: a powerful, worthy, and deserving individual who was capable of achieving anything I set my mind to.

Call To Action

As you read this chapter, I challenge you to pause and reflect on the thoughts that run on autopilot in your mind—the beliefs you've carried with you for so long that you may not even recognize them as limiting. What areas in your life feel stagnant? Where do you feel stuck, like no matter how hard you try, you can't seem to break through? Is it in your finances? Your career? Your relationships?

This stagnation could be a sign of a limiting belief deeply rooted in your subconscious, a belief that is quietly holding you back from achieving the very things you desire. These beliefs often feel like invisible chains—they shape your decisions, your self-worth, and how much you believe you deserve. And the truth is, many of these beliefs were never even yours to begin with. They were handed to you by the experiences of your past, by the words of others and by society's expectations.

But here's the powerful part: once you recognize these limiting beliefs, you have the power to rewrite them. You don't have to stay stuck in the same patterns, feeling like you're not enough. You don't have to settle for less in your relationships, your career, or your finances. You are capable of so much more.

    I invite you today to start noticing the areas in your life where you feel resistance. Ask yourself: What stories am I telling myself about my worth? About what I deserve? About what I'm capable of? Start identifying where those beliefs came from, and challenge them. You were not meant to live a life of limitation—you were meant to step into abundance, power, and purpose. But first, you have to confront the beliefs that are keeping you small.

    Take that first step today. Look inward, face the narrative, and start rewriting your story. The only thing standing between you and the life you truly desire is the belief that you're not worthy of it. It's time to let go of that belief and embrace the truth of who you are: worthy, deserving, and capable of achieving greatness.

Chapter 5: The Dark Side of Pretty Girl Privilege

Everyone talks about the perks of pretty girl privilege—the opportunities that seem to fall into your lap, the attention you receive, the way people treat you differently just because of how you look. It sounds like the dream life, right? But what no one ever talks about is the dark side of this so-called privilege, a side that can leave deep, lasting wounds if you don't learn to protect yourself. A side that, for me, added layers to the already thick shell of limiting beliefs that I carried with me.

No one told me how dangerous it could be to be what the world calls "pretty." No one warned me about the insecure men who would come into my life and try to convince me that I was nothing more than a pretty face and a nice body. These men wanted me to believe that my value was tied solely to my appearance and what I could give them sexually, that I had nothing else to offer. They treated me as though my job was to be pretty, silent, and please them—a trophy to be shown off, but never truly valued.

I became something to be possessed, admired from a distance, but never understood and truly loved. They didn't care about who I really was. They only wanted the image, the fantasy, never the real me. I was something to be experienced, not someone to be known. And in the process, I began to internalize these messages. I began to believe that my worth was indeed tied to my appearance, that I had nothing more to offer the world than my looks and my ability to please a man.

But the men weren't the only ones who contributed to this narrative. The world around me reinforced these beliefs at every turn. No one told me that people, especially women, would look at me and immediately dislike me, putting me in a box based on nothing more than their assumptions. My lighter skin, curvy waist and "good hair" only added fuel to the fire. The one comment I received the most was "I just don't like her. It's something about her". They never had a reason. I was immediately labeled as a gold digger and someone with bad intentions—all without anyone taking the time to get to know the real me.

Even in friendships and family relationships, I couldn't escape the dark side of pretty girl privilege. Some women wanted to befriend me not because they valued who I was, but because they wanted to benefit from the attention I attracted. They knew I was the one who drew the eyes, and they wanted a piece of that spotlight. It wasn't about genuine connection; it was about what they could gain from being associated with me.

One of the most painful experiences came from within my own family. A female family member, someone who was supposed to protect me and guide me in the right direction, instead led me down a path that further eroded my self-worth. She would hook me up with men that she knew was married or taken, completely disregarding the damage this would do to my reputation and my sense of self. I will never forget the night I found out that a man that she had hooked me up with was married with several children. I was crushed! I had been the other woman and didn't even know it. But she did! This betrayal cut deep, reinforcing the belief that I wasn't good enough to have my own husband, that I was destined to be the "other woman," never deserving of true love or commitment.

The challenges didn't stop there. Being beautiful also made it more difficult to find real love. Men were often intimidated by the attention I received, by the idea of being with someone who constantly drew the gaze of others. They had to be extremely secure with themselves to handle the level of attention I attracted, and the truth is, many weren't. A beautiful woman can scare a lot of men away. They might want to experience the fantasy of being with someone beautiful, but when it came to actually being in a committed relationship, it was often too much pressure for them to handle. The very thing that drew them in became the thing that drove them away.

For years, I let these labels define me. I let the world tell me who I was, what I was worth, and where I belonged. The weight of these judgments added to my feelings of inadequacy, reinforcing the limiting beliefs that had been instilled in me from a young age. I began to see myself not through my own eyes, but through the eyes of those who judged me. And in doing so, I lost sight of who I truly was.

But those days are over.

I came to a point where I realized that I had the power to redefine my worth. I had the power to reject the labels that others placed on me and to reclaim my identity. I began to understand that the opinions of others said more about them than they did about me. Most importantly, I learned that I had to protect my beauty—both inner and outer—with everything I had.

Because beauty does come with a dark side. It comes with its own set of rules, challenges, and dangers. And if you don't learn the rule book, you will lose. But beauty is also powerful. It can open doors, create opportunities, and make a lasting impact. The key is learning how to wield it wisely, to protect it, and to protect yourself from those who would try to take advantage of it.

Inspirational Call To Action

In the end, it's not just about being beautiful. It's about being strong, being resilient, and reclaiming your worth in a world that often tries to take it away. It's about recognizing that your value is not determined by your appearance or what you can do for others, but by who you are at your core—your strength, your intelligence, your compassion, your resilience.

So, here's to all the "pretty girls" out there. Your beauty is a gift, but it's not your only gift. Don't let the world define you by it. Protect it, yes, but more importantly, protect yourself. Know your worth, and never let anyone take it away.

Chapter 6: The Art of Personal Development

As I began to break free from the limiting beliefs that had held me back for so long, the journey of reclaiming my power became intertwined with my commitment to personal development. Personal development wasn't just a tool for me; it became a way of life, a guiding force that helped me to rediscover who I truly was and to step into the fullness of my potential.

My background in multi-level marketing had introduced me to the importance of personal growth and having a mentor. In that space, I learned valuable skills and concepts that would later become the foundation of my healing journey. I came to understand that success wasn't just about external achievements—it was about cultivating the right mindset, developing resilience, and continually striving to become the best version of myself.

My healing journey took a significant turn in 2016, when I first watched "The Secret". The concepts presented in that film were like a key that unlocked a new understanding of the world and my place in it. It introduced me to the idea that God had given us gifts. The gift to create a beautiful life using our energy, emotions, and thoughts. That we are not just passive observers of life but active participants who can shape our destiny through the power of our minds and visualization. This was a profound revelation for me, one that resonated deeply with the experiences and beliefs I had been carrying.

From The Secret, I was introduced to the teachings of Napolean Hill, Bob Proctor and Lisa Nichols. These individuals became my virtual mentors, guiding me through the initial stages of my journey towards self-discovery. Bob Proctor's teachings about the subconscious mind and the law of attraction helped me to understand that I was more than just a name, or a person defined by external circumstances—I was energy, vibrations, a powerful being capable of manifesting my desires. Lisa Nichols, with her powerful story of transformation, showed me the importance of owning my story and using it as a tool for empowerment rather than letting it define me in limiting ways.

These teachings were transformative. They helped me to see beyond the limiting beliefs that had held me captive for so long. I began to understand that the barriers I had faced—whether in relationships, career, or finances—were not insurmountable obstacles, but rather reflections of the energy and beliefs onto which I was holding. This understanding was both liberating and empowering. It meant that if I could change my thoughts and my energy, I could change my life.

But this journey of self-discovery did not stop there. Over the years, I continued to seek out mentors and teachings for every area of my life. I found guidance in the words of Eric Thomas, whose motivational speeches ignited a fire within me to keep pushing forward as an entrepreneur, no matter the obstacles. Abraham Hicks introduced me to the concept of alignment and the power of staying in a high vibrational state, where I could attract the things, I wanted into my life with greater ease.

Jay Shetty, with his teachings on mindfulness and purpose, helped me to stay grounded and connected to my true self, even during life's challenges. Laterras Whitfield's Dear. Future Wifey podcast kept my hope for love alive, showing me the beauty of successful marriages and the power of transparency in relationships. RC Blakes Jr. helped me heal the wounds from my father and embrace the mindset of a wife, positioning me to attract the husband meant for me.

These mentors became a vital part of my journey. They were not just voices in books or videos—they were guides who helped me navigate the complexities of my inner world. They taught me the importance of consistency in personal development, the need to continually feed my mind with positivity, and the value of surrounding myself with high-vibrational energy. This daily practice of personal development became my anchor, a way to stay connected to my true self and to keep my energy aligned with my goals and desires.

In addition to studying these mentors, I also embraced the power of high-vibrational music and affirmations. Artist like Tems, Londrelle, Fred Hammond, Yolanda Adams, Perri Jones, Franchesca, Fridayy, Junetober was played on a daily. Music has always been a powerful force in my life, but as I delved deeper into my healing journey, I began to understand its ability to elevate my energy and shift my mindset. I started to incorporate high-vibrational music into my daily routine, using it as a tool to lift my spirits, boost my energy, and keep me in a positive state of mind. Alongside this, I practiced daily affirmations, speaking words of power and positivity over my life, reinforcing the beliefs I wanted to embody.

Reclaiming my power was not just about shedding old beliefs—it was about actively cultivating new ones. It was about replacing the old narrative of unworthiness with a new story of empowerment, abundance, and limitless potential. This process was ongoing, requiring daily commitment and effort, but it was also incredibly rewarding. With each day, I felt myself growing stronger, more aligned with my true self, and more confident in my ability to create the life I desired.

Call To Action

Personal development isn't just a tool—it's a way of life. It's the process of becoming the best version of yourself by consistently feeding your mind, body, and soul with the energy and information that will help you grow. I've learned that true transformation doesn't happen by accident—it's intentional. It requires you to show up for yourself every day, to commit to your growth, and to be willing to confront the beliefs that are holding you back.

I challenge you today to take ownership of your personal development journey. Whether you're just starting out or have been on this path for a while, there's always another level of growth waiting for you. Ask yourself: What am I feeding my mind daily? What energy am I allowing into my space? Personal development isn't about perfection; it's about progress. It's about making the choice, day after day, to invest in yourself, to surround yourself with positivity, and to keep moving forward, even when the journey gets tough.

Look at the mentors and guides who resonate with you, whether it's through books, podcasts, or videos. Let their stories and teachings fuel your own growth. And don't forget the power of the simple tools at your disposal—high-vibrational music, affirmations, and moments of stillness. These are your anchors, helping you stay aligned with the person you are becoming.

This is your journey to reclaim your power. To break free from the limiting beliefs that have held you back and to step into the fullness of who you were always meant to be. You are not limited by your past. You are not bound by your circumstances. You have the power to create the life you desire, starting today.

So, I encourage you—make that commitment to yourself. Dive deep into your personal development, and watch as your life begins to transform in ways you never imagined.

Chapter 7: The Only Way Out Is In

Mentors, therapist, and counselors are great. But they cannot and will not replace the work that MUST be done on the inside. They are only a guide.

The turning point of change came when I began to realize that the only way to break free from the cycle of self-sacrifice and unworthiness was to turn inward. See, for so long, I had looked to others to validate my worth, to tell me who I was and what I was worth.

But no matter how much I tried, I could never find the validation I was seeking because I was looking in the wrong place. The answers I was searching for couldn't be found outside of myself—they had to come from within.

This realization didn't come overnight—it was a slow, gradual process that unfolded over time. The first step was acknowledging that I had been living my life based on lies and a set of beliefs that weren't true. I had believed for so long that I wasn't in control of my life or my worthiness. I thought I had to prove myself to others to be worthy of love and attention. But during my journey inward, I realized this wasn't true. I knew that I was worthy simply because I existed, that I didn't have to do anything to earn love or validation. This realization was both liberating and terrifying. It meant letting go of the need to prove myself, which had been a driving force in my life for so long. It meant trusting that I was enough just as I was, without having to do anything to earn it.

As I began to explore this new way of thinking, I started to connect with my true self—the part of me that had been silenced for so long. I began to listen to that small, quiet voice inside of me, the one that knew my worth and didn't need external validation. This voice became stronger as I began to nurture it, and it guided me on a journey inward, a journey of self-discovery and healing.

One of the most important lessons I learned on this journey was the power of self-compassion and Grace. For so long, I had been my own worst critic, constantly berating myself for not being good enough and making the right decisions.

But as I began to turn inward, I realized that I needed to be kinder to myself, to treat myself with the same compassion and understanding that I would offer to a friend. I also had to remind myself that if I knew better, I would have done better. This was a difficult shift to make, as it went against everything, I had been taught to believe about myself. But slowly, I began to practice self-compassion, learning to forgive myself for my perceived shortcomings and to embrace my imperfections.

Another key aspect of my journey inward was learning to set boundaries. I had spent so much of my life giving to others, often at the expense of my own well-being. But as

I began to connect with my true self, I realized that I needed to protect my energy and prioritize my own needs. Setting boundaries wasn't easy, especially when it meant saying no to people who were used to me always saying yes. But it was a necessary step in reclaiming my power and taking control of my life.

As I continued this journey, I began to see myself in a new light. I was no longer defined by the limiting beliefs that had held me back for so long. Instead, I began to see myself as a whole, worthy, and deserving individual. This shift in perspective did not happen overnight, and it wasn't without its challenges. There were moments of doubt and fear, times when I questioned whether I was truly worthy of love and happiness. But each time, I came back to that small, quiet voice inside of me, the one that knew the truth.

The journey inward was not just about healing the wounds of the past—it was about creating a new foundation for my life. It was about reclaiming my power and stepping into my true self, the self that had always been there, waiting for me to acknowledge it. This journey was not easy, and it required me to face some of the darkest parts of myself. But it was also incredibly rewarding, as it allowed me to break free from the chains of my limiting beliefs and step into the fullness of who I truly was that I was worthy of love and happiness, simply because I existed.

Call To Action

As I reflect on the turning point in my life—the moment when I stopped seeking validation from others and began to turn inward—I'm reminded of the incredible power that lies within each of us. We spend so much of our lives looking outside of ourselves for love, validation, and worth. But the truth is, the answers we seek can only be found by turning inward, by connecting with the part of us that has always known our true value.

I challenge you to ask yourself: Where have I been seeking validation? In my relationships? In my career? In the approval of others?

Now take a moment to imagine what it would feel like to let go of that need. To stop seeking outside validation and instead, listen to the quiet voice inside you—the one that has always known you are enough, simply because you exist.

This journey inward isn't easy. It requires you to face the parts of yourself you've been avoiding, the parts you've been too afraid to confront. But this is where true healing begins. It's in the stillness, in the moments of self-reflection, that you can begin to rewrite the story you've been telling yourself for so long. The story that says you're not enough, that you have to prove your worth, that you have to sacrifice your own well-being to be loved.

It's time to challenge that story. It's time to embrace self-compassion, to treat yourself with the grace and kindness you've been giving to everyone else. Set boundaries, protect your energy, and begin to prioritize your own needs. This is not selfish—it's necessary. You cannot pour from an empty cup.

I invite you today to begin your journey inward. Take that first step. Turn down the noise of the outside world and listen to what your heart has been trying to tell you all along: You are worthy. You are enough. And you always have been.

Chapter 8: Living in Alignment

As I reclaimed my power and embraced personal development as a way of life, I began to experience what it truly meant to live in alignment. Living in alignment wasn't just a concept—it was a daily practice, a commitment to staying true to myself, my values, and my purpose. It meant making choices that resonated with my inner truth, rather than being swayed by external expectations or fears.

One of the key aspects of living in alignment was maintaining a high vibrational state. This was very important. I had learned through my studies that our energy is one of the most powerful tools we have for creating the life we desire. When we are in a high vibrational state—feeling joy, love, gratitude, and positivity—we attract more of those same energies into our lives. This understanding became a guiding principle for me as I navigated the ups and downs of life.

To maintain this high vibrational state, I made it a priority to feed myself with positivity every day. This meant starting my mornings with an attitude of gratitude finding something to be grateful for. It also included personal development, listening to my mentors' teachings, reading uplifting books, and setting intentions for the day. It meant incorporating high-vibrational music into my routine, using it to elevate my mood and keep my energy aligned with my goals. I found that these practices not only helped me to stay positive, but they also created a ripple effect in other areas of my life, attracting opportunities, relationships, and experiences that were in harmony with my desires.

Living in alignment also required me to be intentional about my actions and decisions. I had to continually check in with myself to ensure that the choices I was making were truly aligned with my values and purpose. This meant saying no to opportunities that didn't feel right, even if they seemed promising on the surface. It meant setting boundaries with people who drained my energy or didn't support my growth. And it meant being honest with myself about what I truly wanted, rather than settling for what was comfortable or expected.

One of the most powerful aspects of living in alignment was the way it changed my relationship with success and abundance. I no longer saw success as something I had to chase or prove myself worthy of. Instead, I began to see it as a natural byproduct of living in alignment with my true self. When I was aligned with myself and God, success flowed to me with ease. Opportunities appeared, clients valued my work, and financial abundance became a reflection of the value I was bringing into the world.

This shift in perspective was incredible. It allowed me to let go of the need to constantly strive or struggle, and instead, to trust that I was exactly where I needed to be. I began to see challenges not as obstacles, but as opportunities for growth and learning. I started to approach life with a sense of curiosity and openness, knowing that as long as I stayed aligned with my true self and kept a strong relationship with God, everything else would fall into place.

Living in alignment also deepened my connection with my intuition. I began to trust my inner guidance more fully, recognizing that it was always leading me towards my highest good. This trust allowed me to make decisions with confidence, even when the path ahead wasn't entirely clear. I knew that as long as I stayed true to myself and followed my intuition, I would always be supported and guided in the right direction.

Over time, living in alignment became second nature to me. It wasn't just something I practiced occasionally—it was the foundation of my life. It shaped how I approached my work, my relationships, and my personal growth. It allowed me to live with greater purpose, joy, and fulfillment, knowing that I was creating a life that was truly my own.

Living in alignment wasn't without its challenges, but it was the most rewarding journey I had ever embarked on. It allowed me to step into my power, to embrace my true self, and to create a life that was rich in meaning and purpose. It was a journey of continual growth, evolution, and discovery—one that I was committed to for the rest of my life.

Call To Action

Living in alignment isn't just a practice—it's a way of life, a commitment to honoring who you truly are. It's about aligning your actions, your thoughts, and your energy with the highest version of yourself. But here's the truth: alignment requires intentionality. It requires daily decisions, daily check-ins with yourself, and the courage to choose what resonates with your inner truth, even when it's not the easiest path.

So, I ask you, where in your life are you living out of alignment? Are you making decisions based on fear, external expectations, or comfort? Or are you truly honoring your values and your purpose with every choice you make?

This is your invitation to take a step back, reflect, and start living in alignment. Pay attention to how you feel when you make decisions—does it feel light and joyful, or heavy and draining? Your feelings are powerful indicators of whether you're in alignment or not.

I challenge you today to make one decision that brings you into greater alignment with your true self. It could be setting a boundary, saying no to an opportunity that doesn't feel right, or simply starting your day with gratitude and intention. Remember, when you align with your highest self, the universe moves in your favor. You don't have to chase success, love, or abundance—it will flow to you effortlessly when you're living in alignment.

Take that first step today. Commit to feeding your mind, body, and soul with high vibrational energy. Trust your intuition, set your intentions, and know that as long as you stay true to yourself, you are always on the right path.

Chapter 9: The Power of Stillness

As I continued my journey toward alignment, I discovered the power of stillness and solitude. However, my path to embracing stillness wasn't conventional—it was deeply personal and adapted to the unique circumstances of my life. I realized early on that stillness didn't have to look a certain way; it didn't require a perfect setting, a dedicated meditation space, or even complete silence. Stillness, I found, was about creating a space where I could connect with my inner self, no matter where I was or what was happening around me.

My journey with meditation began in a way that was uniquely my own. With a young child to care for, I had to find creative ways to carve out time for myself. My son was just 2 years old at the time, and the only moments of quiet I could find were early in the morning, before he woke up. These quiet moments became sacred to me. I would retreat to the bathroom, not because it was an ideal meditation space, but because it was the only place, I could go without being disturbed. I didn't have the luxury of a meditation room or a perfectly curated environment, but I made do with what I had.

In that small bathroom, I found my sanctuary. I would sit on the floor, listening to nature sounds or Bob Proctor's abundance meditations. The gentle flow of water, the rustling of leaves, the distant call of birds—these sounds helped me to center myself, to tune out the noise of the world, and to focus on the stillness within. I discovered that nature's rhythms had a calming effect on me, allowing my mind to settle and my thoughts to become more focused.

On the bathroom mirror, I had posted affirmations—powerful, positive statements that reminded me of my worth, my goals, and the life I was striving to create. As I meditated, I would repeat these affirmations to myself, allowing them to sink deep into my subconscious. One of my favorite affirmations was "Money comes easily and frequently & Everything is always working out for me". & I would visualize my goals with as much detail as I could muster, imagining what my life would look like when I achieved them, feeling the emotions of success, joy, and fulfillment as if they were already mine.

These moments of stillness in the early morning became a time of creation for me. I realized that meditation wasn't just about quieting the mind; it was an opportunity to visualize and create the life I desired. It was a space where I could connect with God, where I could hear His voice guiding me, where I could align my energy with my highest aspirations.

Stillness, I discovered, was essential for hearing God's voice, for receiving divine inspiration, and for visualizing the path ahead. No matter what you call it—meditation, prayer, stillness—it was in these quiet moments that I found the clarity and guidance I needed to move forward.

As my journey continued, my meditation practice evolved. I no longer needed to retreat to the bathroom in the early morning hours. Instead, I found a new sanctuary in the gym. Every morning, like clockwork, I wake up at 5 AM and head to the gym. This routine became more than just a workout—it was an appointment with God. The act of moving my body, of pushing myself physically, seemed to enhance my mental clarity and open a channel of communication with the divine.

During these early morning workouts, I experienced some of my most profound insights. It's as if the physical exertion clears away the mental clutter, allowing me to hear God's voice more clearly. Ideas flow to me effortlessly, solutions to problems present themselves, and I feel a deep sense of connection and alignment with my purpose. There's something about moving while meditating, about combining physical activity with mental focus, that enhances the entire experience. It's as if my body and mind are working in harmony, creating a powerful synergy that elevates my meditation practice to a new level.

If I ever miss a morning at the gym, I feel as though I've missed an important appointment. It's not just about missing a workout—it's about missing that sacred time with God, that time of stillness and connection that sets the tone for the rest of my day. The gym has become my temple, my place of worship, where I not only strengthen my body but also nourish my soul.

Through these personal experiences, I've come to

understand that stillness can take many forms. It doesn't have to fit a specific mold or follow a particular set of rules. Whether it's sitting in a bathroom at dawn, listening to nature sounds, or moving my body in the gym, stillness is about creating a space where I can connect with my inner self, hear God's voice, and visualize the life I want to create. It's about finding what works for me, what resonates with my soul, and using that to guide my journey of self-discovery and alignment.

Call To Action

Stillness isn't about having the perfect environment or setting aside hours of your day—it's about creating a sacred space, wherever you are, to connect with yourself and with God. It's about allowing yourself the time to pause, to reflect, and to simply be. It's the time to reflect on your thoughts, behaviors and feelings. It's the time to "Think about what you're thinking about". In this world of constant noise and distraction, stillness is your most powerful tool for gaining clarity, receiving guidance, and aligning with your true self.

So, I invite you today to ask yourself: Where is my space for stillness? You don't need a meditation room or complete silence. It can be wherever you find peace—whether it's in your home, a walk in nature, or even during your morning commute. The important thing is to create a moment for yourself, a moment where you can listen to your heart, your thoughts, and the divine guidance that is always available to you.

Stillness is where you can hear God's voice. It's

where you can visualize the life you desire, where you can realign your energy and purpose. I challenge you to make time today, no matter how busy you are, to create a space of stillness. Take five minutes, close your eyes, focus on your breath, and think about what you're thinking about. Reflect on the thoughts that are driving your life and ask yourself if they're in alignment with your highest good.

In those moments of stillness, you have the power to create, to connect, and to reset your energy. You don't have to wait for the perfect time or place. Start right now. Your space for stillness is waiting for you, and in it, you'll find the clarity and guidance you've been seeking."

Chapter 10: The Art of Transformation

As I journeyed deeper into alignment with my true self, I began to understand that transformation is not a one-time event—it is an ongoing process, a continual evolution that requires dedication, self-awareness, and a willingness to embrace change. The more I committed to my personal growth, the more I realized that transformation was an art—an art that required practice, patience, and a deep understanding of the self.

At the core of this transformation was the realization that mind, body, and spirit are deeply interconnected. If I wanted to experience true, lasting change, I had to address all aspects of my being. Meditation and personal development had been central to my transformation, but I realized that my health played an equally crucial role. The state of my body was directly tied to the state of my mind and spirit. The more I took care of my physical health, the clearer my mind became, and the more I could connect with my inner guidance.

I began to make changes to my diet, understanding that what I put into my body had a direct impact on how

I felt, both physically and mentally. I decided to cut out all meat from my diet and reduce my sugar intake. These changes weren't always easy, and I wasn't perfect in my approach, but even small adjustments made a significant difference. As I started to eat cleaner, my mind became clearer, and I found it easier to focus, to hear God's voice, and to stay aligned with my goals. My physical health improved, and with it came a sense of empowerment—knowing that I was taking control of my life from the inside out.

But physical health wasn't the only transformation I needed to embrace. There was another, equally important, obstacle that I had to overcome: fear. Just as my diet had once clouded my mind, fear had been clouding my decisions. Fear of failure, fear of judgment, fear of not being good enough. For so long, fear had held me back, whispering doubts in my ear, telling me that I wasn't capable, that I would fail if I tried to step out of my comfort zone.

As I took steps to clear out the physical clutter from my life, I realized that I had to do the same with fear. I had to stop entertaining it, stop allowing it to take up space in my mind. This wasn't an easy process—overcoming fear required me to confront the deeply ingrained beliefs that had kept me stuck for so long. But I was determined to break free from its grip.

The more I let go of fear, the more I realized that failure was not something to be feared—it was something to be embraced. Failure became a steppingstone to success, a necessary part of the learning process. Just as I had cleaned up my diet to clear my mind, I had to clear out my fears to open myself up to new opportunities. With each failure, I grew stronger, more confident, and more aligned with my purpose.

As my physical health improved, so did my mental clarity and emotional resilience. The fear that once held me back began to dissolve, replaced by a sense of empowerment and possibility. I no longer saw failure as a setback, but as a natural part of my journey—a necessary experience that propelled me forward.

Transformation, I realized, is not about focusing on just one part of your life. It's about addressing the whole self—mind, body, and spirit—and embracing growth in all its forms. The changes I made to my health were not just physical; they created a ripple effect that touched every aspect of my life. As I became healthier, I became bolder, more confident, and more willing to take risks. As I let go of fear, I stepped into a new version of myself—one that was strong, capable, and unafraid to fail.

Ultimately, the art of transformation is about clearing out the old to make way for the new, about facing fears head-on, and about committing to the ongoing journey of becoming the best version of yourself. It's about realizing that transformation is not a destination—it's a lifelong journey, one that requires continual dedication, self-awareness, and a deep commitment to living in alignment with your true self.

Call To Action

Transformation isn't a one-time event—it's a journey, a process of continually evolving into the best version of yourself. And here's the truth: that transformation starts with you. It starts with the choices you make every single day—what you feed your body, what you feed your mind, and how you respond to fear.

I challenge you today to take a moment and reflect. What areas of your life need transformation? Is it your health? Your mindset? Your fears? Remember, transformation is not just about changing one thing—it's about addressing the whole self.

Start small. Make one decision today that aligns with the version of yourself you want to become. Maybe it's choosing healthier food. Maybe it's taking a step towards facing a fear you've been avoiding. Whatever it is, commit to it. Embrace the process of growth, even when it feels uncomfortable, because that's where the magic happens.

The art of transformation is about taking small, consistent steps in the direction of your dreams. It's about trusting that you are capable of becoming everything you desire to be. The journey may not be easy, but it's worth it. You are worth it. Start today. Take the first step, and watch as your life begins to transform from the inside out.

Chapter 11: The Ripple Effect of Transformation

As I moved further along my path of transformation, I began to notice the ripple effect it had on every aspect of my life. Transformation, I realized, happens in isolation but it doesn't remain—it extends outward, touching everything and everyone around you. The changes I made within myself began to manifest in my family, relationships, my work, and the opportunities that came my way. The more I aligned with my true self, the more the world around me seemed to align with who I was becoming.

One of the most significant ripple effects was in my relationships. As I transformed, I began to attract people who resonated with my new energy. These were individuals who supported my growth, who inspired me, and who were also on their own journeys of transformation. My relationships became deeper, more meaningful, and more authentic. I found myself surrounded by people who lifted me up, who challenged me to keep growing, and who saw me for who I truly was, not for who I had been.

This shift in relationships wasn't always easy. As I evolved, there were people in my life who were no longer aligned with the person I was becoming. Some relationships faded away naturally, while others required difficult conversations and intentional decisions to create distance. Letting go of these relationships was painful, but necessary.

I knew that in order to continue growing, I needed to surround myself with people who were in alignment with my values and my vision for the future. This process of letting go was an act of self-love and self-respect, a way of honoring the person I was becoming and creating space for new, supportive connections to enter my life.

The ripple effect of my transformation also extended to my work. As I became more aligned with my true self, I found that my work began to reflect this alignment. Opportunities that were in harmony with my passions and values started to flow into my life.

I no longer had to chase success or force things to happen—success came to me naturally, as a result of living in alignment with my purpose. My work became more fulfilling, more impactful, and more enjoyable. I was doing what I loved, in a way that felt authentic to me, and the results spoke for themselves.

This alignment in my work also led to greater financial abundance. As I let go of the limiting beliefs that had once held me back, I found myself open to receiving more. I began to charge what I was truly worth, to set boundaries around my time and energy, and to attract clients and opportunities that valued my skills and expertise. Financial success was no longer something I had to strive for—it became a natural outcome of living in alignment with my true self.

Another powerful ripple effect of my transformation was the impact it had on my sense of purpose. The more I aligned with my true self, the clearer my purpose became. I began to see how everything I had experienced—both the challenges and the triumphs—had been preparing me for the work I was meant to do in the world. My purpose wasn't something I had to find or create—it was something that was already within me, waiting to be uncovered and expressed.

This sense of purpose gave my life new meaning. It guided my decisions, shaped my goals, and fueled my passion for personal growth and helping others. I knew that my journey of transformation wasn't just about me—it was about using my experiences, my insights, and my gifts to make a positive impact on the world. This purpose-driven life brought me a deep sense of fulfillment and joy, and it inspired me to keep growing, learning, and evolving.

As I continued to embrace the ripple effect of transformation, I also became more aware of the impact my energy had on others. I realized that my thoughts, beliefs, and actions didn't just affect me—they influenced the people around me as well. When I operated from a place of fear, doubt, or negativity, that energy would ripple out and affect those I interacted with. But when I operated from a place of love, positivity, and alignment, that energy would also ripple out, creating a positive impact on those around me.

This awareness deepened my commitment to living in alignment with my true self. I wanted to be a source of positive energy, a force for good in the world. I wanted my presence to uplift others, to inspire them to see the best in themselves, and to encourage them on their own journeys of transformation. This wasn't just about personal growth—it was about making a difference in the lives of others, one interaction at a time.

Call To Action

Transformation isn't just about changing yourself—it's about creating a ripple effect that touches every part of your life and the lives of those around you. As you grow, evolve, and align with your true self, you become a source of positive energy, influencing the world in ways you may not even realize.

So today, I challenge you to reflect on the ripple effect of your own transformation. How has your personal growth impacted your relationships? Your work? Your sense of purpose? Every decision you make, every belief you hold, and every action you take has the power to create waves that extend far beyond yourself.

Ask yourself: What kind of ripple effect am I creating? Are you lifting others up, inspiring them to see the best in themselves, or are you allowing fear, doubt, or negativity to influence those around you? Remember, your energy is contagious. When you live in alignment with your true self, you not only transform your own life—you become a light for others, encouraging them on their own journey of growth.

Let this be your reminder that your transformation is not just about you. It's about the impact you're making in the world. So, continue to live in alignment, continue to embrace your purpose, and watch as the ripple effect of your transformation creates positive change in ways you never thought possible.

Chapter 12: Embracing the Journey

One of the most important lessons I've learned on this journey is the power of acceptance. In the past, I often struggled with accepting where I was in life, always wanting to be further ahead, always striving for the next achievement or goal. But as I've grown, I've come to realize that true transformation requires acceptance—acceptance of where you are, acceptance of the process, and acceptance of the pace at which your journey unfolds.

This doesn't mean giving up on your goals or settling for less than what you desire. Rather, it means acknowledging that every step of the journey is important, that every experience has value, and that growth takes time. It means trusting that you are exactly where you need to be, even if it doesn't always feel like it. Acceptance allows you to release the pressure to be perfect, to let go of the need to control every outcome, and to find peace in the present moment.

Embracing the journey also means being kind to yourself along the way. Transformation can be challenging—it requires you to confront your fears, to step out of your comfort zone, and to face parts of yourself that you may have been avoiding. There will be setbacks, mistakes, and moments of doubt. But these are all part of the process. The key is to treat yourself with compassion, to celebrate your progress, and to keep moving forward, even when the path is difficult.

Another crucial aspect of embracing the journey is staying open to change. Transformation is not a linear process—it's a dynamic, ever-evolving experience that requires flexibility and adaptability. As you grow, your goals, desires, and values may change. What once served you may no longer be in alignment with who you are becoming. This is natural and part of the journey. Staying open to change means being willing to let go of what no longer serves you and to embrace new opportunities, new ways of thinking, and new paths that align with your true self.

As I continued on my journey, I also learned the importance of staying connected to my vision and purpose. In the midst of change and growth, it can be easy to lose sight of why you started the journey in the first place. But staying connected to your vision and purpose serves as a guiding light, helping you navigate the challenges and uncertainties that may arise. It reminds you of what truly matters, of the impact you want to make, and of the life you are committed to creating.

For me, staying connected to my vision and purpose meant regularly revisiting my goals, reflecting on my progress, and reminding myself of why I was on this journey. It meant surrounding myself with people who supported my growth, who shared my values, and who encouraged me to keep moving forward. It meant continuing to invest in my personal development, to learn from mentors and teachers who inspired me, and to stay committed to the practices that kept me aligned with my true self.

One of the most rewarding aspects of embracing the journey has been the opportunity to share my experiences with others. As I've grown and transformed, I've been able to use my story to inspire and empower others on their own journeys. I've shared the lessons I've learned, the strategies that have helped me, and the insights that have guided me along the way. This has not only been fulfilling for me, but it has also reinforced the idea that our journeys are not just about ourselves—they are about making a positive impact on the world around us.

In embracing the journey, I've also learned to find joy in the process. It's easy to get caught up in the destination, to focus solely on where you want to be and to miss the beauty of where you are right now. But transformation is about more than just reaching your goals—it's about finding fulfillment in the daily steps you take toward those goals. It's about appreciating the small victories, the moments of growth, and the experiences that shape who you are becoming. When you can find joy in the journey, the destination becomes even more rewarding.

As I continue this path of transformation, I know that the journey is far from over. There will always be new challenges to face, new lessons to learn, and new levels of growth to achieve. But I am committed to embracing the journey, to staying true to myself, and to living a life that is rich in purpose, meaning, and fulfillment.

Inspirational Call to Action

One of the biggest lessons I've learned is that it's so easy to compare your journey to someone else's, to look at where you are and feel like you're not doing enough, not moving fast enough, not achieving what you see others have already accomplished. I used to do that all the time—comparing my chapter 2 to someone else's chapter 50. I would ask myself, Why am I not there yet? Why haven't I achieved what I've been working so hard for?

But here's the truth I had to learn: just because you're not where you want to be right now doesn't mean you're not on the right path. God's timing is perfect, and sometimes, what feels like a delay is really just preparation. I used to ask for success, thinking I was ready. But looking back, I realize that if I had gotten what I wanted when I asked for it, I wouldn't have been able to handle it. Can you imagine achieving everything you've ever dreamed of, but not having the boundaries or strength to sustain it? That's how much God loves you—He won't give you something you're not ready for, because He knows it would overwhelm you, not bless you.

So, if you're feeling like you're not where you should be, if you're comparing yourself to others, I challenge you to shift your perspective. Trust that God hears your prayers, but He's also preparing you for what you're asking for. Understand that your worth isn't measured by how quickly you achieve your goals—it's measured by your ability to embrace the process, to learn, to grow, and to trust in God's timing.

You are not behind. You are exactly where you need to be. And when the time is right, when you are fully prepared, God will open the doors you've been praying for. Until then, embrace the journey, knowing that every step you take is getting you closer to where you're meant to be. Keep trusting, keep growing, and know that the best is yet to come.

Chapter 13: The Foundation of Faith

As I look back on my journey of transformation, I realize that none of it would have been possible without the foundation of faith. Faith wasn't just a part of my journey—it was the bedrock upon which everything else was built. It was the anchor that kept me grounded in moments of uncertainty, the guiding light that led me through the darkest times, and the force that propelled me forward when I couldn't see the way ahead.

From the very beginning, my faith was tested in ways I never could have imagined. God called me to fulfill assignments that were far beyond anything I had ever dreamed of or planned for. He gave me visions—clear, undeniable glimpses of what He wanted me to do, the programs He wanted me to implement, and the impact He wanted me to have on the world. These visions were overwhelming at times, and I often found myself wondering, "Why me? How am I supposed to do this?"

The magnitude of the tasks before me was daunting. There were moments when I felt completely unqualified, moments when I questioned whether I was really hearing God's voice or just my own imagination. But each time doubt crept in, I was reminded that faith is not about having all the answers—it's about trusting in God's plan, even when it doesn't make sense. It's about stepping out in obedience, even when you can't see the full picture.

Faith required me to trust in God's timing and His provision. There were countless times when I didn't know how I would find the resources, the people, or the opportunities to bring these visions to life. But each time, I chose to lean on my faith, to believe that if God had called me to this mission, He would also provide everything I needed to fulfill it. And time and time again, He did. Doors that I never could have opened on my own began to swing wide, and opportunities that seemed impossible suddenly became reality.

This wasn't just about believing in a higher power—it was about believing in the purpose that God had placed within me. It was about understanding that I was a vessel for something much greater than myself, that my life had been orchestrated for a reason, and that I had been chosen to carry out these assignments because God saw something in me that I couldn't yet see in myself.

Faith also required me to surrender my plans and expectations to God. I had to let go of the need to control every detail, to know every step of the journey before I took it. Instead, I had to learn to walk by faith, trusting that God was guiding my steps even when the path was unclear. This wasn't easy for someone like me, who had always been so determined to achieve and succeed. But as I released my need for control, I found a new sense of peace and freedom.

I realized that I didn't have to carry the weight of the world on my shoulders—God was carrying it for me.

Through faith, I began to see the challenges and obstacles in my life in a new light. They were no longer barriers—they were opportunities for growth, for learning, and for deepening my relationship with God. Each challenge was a chance to exercise my faith, to trust that God was working all things together for my good, even when I couldn't see how. This shift in perspective allowed me to approach life with a sense of calm and confidence, knowing that God was with me every step of the way.

Inspirational Call to Action

Faith is the foundation of everything. It's the bedrock that supports you when nothing else makes sense, when the vision seems too big, and when doubt tries to take over. I remember so clearly the moment God called me to start the Mental-ship Program for Teens and the Cultural Exchange Program in Uganda. At the time, I felt unqualified—who was I to lead these initiatives? I had made so many mistakes, taken so many wrong turns, and I couldn't understand why God would choose me.

But here's the thing about faith—it's not about having it all together. It's not about being perfect or knowing every step ahead. It's about trusting that if God has called you to something, He will provide everything you need to fulfill it. And that's exactly what He did. I started those programs on pure faith, without knowing where the resources would come from, but trusting that if this was God's assignment, He would make a way. And here we are, three years later, running both programs successfully.

God won't fund your plans—He will only fund His. So, if you're feeling called to something that feels bigger than you, if you're wondering how, it will all come together, remember this: Faith is the currency that moves mountains. Trust that God has chosen you for a reason, even if you can't see it yet. Step out in faith, knowing that God's plans are already in motion, and that He will provide every resource, every opportunity, and every open door you need.

I challenge you today to take that step of faith. Whatever vision God has placed in your heart, trust that He will bring it to life. You don't have to have it all figured out—you just have to say yes. Let faith be your foundation, and watch as God turns the impossible into reality.

Chapter 14: The Power of Obedience

While faith was the foundation of my journey, obedience was the action that brought it all to life. Faith without action is incomplete, and obedience is the manifestation of that faith in the physical world. It's the willingness to say "yes" to God's call, even when it's uncomfortable, even when it doesn't make sense, and even when it requires stepping into the unknown.

When God began to give me visions and instructions, I knew that I had a choice to make. I could either shrink back in fear and doubt, or I could step forward in obedience, trusting that God would guide me and provide for me along the way. I chose obedience, not because it was easy, but because I knew that this was the path God had laid out for me. And once I made that choice, everything began to change.

Obedience was not just about following instructions—it was about aligning my will with God's will. It was about surrendering my desires, my plans, and my timing to Him, and trusting that His plan was far greater than anything I could imagine. This required a level of humility and trust that I had never experienced before. It meant letting go of my ego, my need for control, and my fear of failure, and allowing God to lead the way.

One of the most challenging aspects of obedience was stepping into roles and assignments that I felt completely unprepared for. There were times when God called me to do things that were far outside of my comfort zone—things that I had never done before and had no idea how to accomplish. But each time, I reminded myself that God doesn't call the equipped—He equips the called. And as I stepped out in obedience, I began to see that God was equipping me with everything I needed, exactly when I needed it.

Obedience also required a deep level of trust in God's timing. There were moments when I wanted to move faster, to see results immediately, but God taught me the importance of patience and waiting on His perfect timing. I learned that obedience is not just about taking action—it's about being in sync with God's timing, about moving when He says move and waiting when He says wait.

This was a difficult lesson for me, but it was also one of the most valuable. It taught me that God's timing is always perfect, and that when I align my actions with His timing, everything falls into place.

As I continued to walk in obedience, I began to see the doors of heaven open in ways I never could have imagined. Opportunities began to flow into my life with ease, connections were made that I never could have orchestrated on my own, and resources appeared just when I needed them. It was as if God was waiting for me to prove my obedience before releasing the full scope of my mission. And once

I did, He poured out His blessings in abundance.

Obedience also brought a deep sense of fulfillment and peace. There's a unique joy that comes from knowing that you are walking in alignment with God's will, that you are fulfilling the purpose He has placed.

Inspirational Call to Action

Faith without action is incomplete. Obedience is the key that unlocks the doors to God's promises—it's where your faith comes alive. Obedience isn't always comfortable, it's not always easy, but it's the step that turns belief into reality. It's saying 'yes' to God, even when you don't have all the answers, even when the road ahead is unclear.

Even during the moments, I felt unqualified, unprepared, and unsure, I still chose obedience, and with every step, God equipped me with exactly what I needed. And here's the beautiful truth: God doesn't call the equipped—He equips the called. When you step out in obedience, He provides, He opens doors, and He brings resources into your life that you never could have imagined.

Today, I challenge you to listen to God's call on your life. What is He asking of you? What vision has He placed in your heart? It may feel overwhelming but remember that your role is to say 'yes' and trust that God will handle the rest. You don't have to know every detail. You just need to take the first step, trusting that God will guide you every step of the way.

Obedience is about more than just following instructions—it's about aligning your will with God's, trusting in His timing, and moving when He says move. There is power in obedience, and when you fully surrender to it, you'll see doors open in ways you never imagined. Identify an area where you feel called to act and take a step in obedience and watch how God moves in your life.

Chapter 15: The Power of Connections

One of the most incredible truths I've learned on this journey is that when you walk in faith and obedience, God doesn't just give you the vision—He also gives you the connections you need to bring that vision to life. When you trust Him and take the steps, He's laid out for you, He opens doors that you could never open on your own. He aligns the right people at the right time to help you carry out His plans.

Looking back, I can see so many moments where God orchestrated divine connections that I never could have predicted. One of the most powerful examples of this came when I was involved in multi-level marketing. This was more than just a business opportunity—it became a training ground where I learned invaluable skills in leadership, personal development, and networking. But more importantly, it was where I met Lisa Nicole Cloud, a woman who would play a key role in the connections that led to the creation of my Cultural Exchange Program in Uganda.

Lisa Nicole Cloud, known as the "Millionaire Maker," is a leader in the multi-level marketing industry, and you may know her from the Bravo show Married to Medicine.

Back in 2019, she held a conference called the Women's Empowerment Network (WEN). It was an event designed to uplift and empower women in business, and I was honored to be a VIP guest speaker at that event. I didn't know it at the time, but this would be a pivotal moment in my journey.

At the conference, I not only had the opportunity to share my story and inspire others, but I also made a connection that would change the trajectory of my work. Among the other guest speakers was a woman who had deep ties to Africa and had been doing work on the continent for years. As we began to talk, she shared with me her experiences and the work she had been doing in Africa. It was a powerful connection because at that point, God had already planted the seed in my heart to start a Cultural Exchange Program, but I had no idea how I was going to make it happen.

This woman became a bridge—she introduced me to the right people, the contacts I needed to make my vision a reality. Through her, I met individuals who had the experience and resources to help me implement the program. It was as if every conversation, every introduction, and every step was part of a divine plan, carefully orchestrated by God. All the dots began to connect, and what had once seemed impossible became not only possible but tangible.

When I look back on that experience, I can see so clearly how faith and obedience led me to that moment. If I hadn't trusted God and stepped into the opportunities He placed before me, I never would have been in that room. I never would have met the people who helped bring the Cultural Exchange Program to life. This is how God works—when you're walking in faith, He aligns you with the right people at the right time, ensuring that His vision will come to fruition.

It's all connected. Every experience, every person, and every opportunity was part of a larger plan. And what's so beautiful is that this wasn't a one-time thing. Throughout my journey, I've seen time and time again how God brings the right connections into my life when I need them most. Whether it's for the Mental-ship Program for teens or the work I'm doing in Africa, God has always provided the people, resources, and opportunities to carry out His plans.

This chapter of my journey is a testament to the power of connections—divine connections that can only come when you walk in obedience and trust God's timing. If you've been given a vision that feels too big or overwhelming, I encourage you to trust that God has already aligned the people and resources you need. You don't have to have it all figured out. Just take the next step in faith, and watch as God brings the right connections into your life to make His vision a reality.

Call to Action

Let me remind you—God's vision for your life is far greater than what you could ever imagine. But here's the beauty of walking in faith and obedience: you don't have to make it all happen on your own.

God is already orchestrating the connections, aligning the right people, and opening the doors that will bring His vision to life. Your job is to trust Him, take that next step, and allow Him to guide the process.

If there's a vision that feels too big, too overwhelming, or impossible to achieve, know that you're not walking this path alone. Divine connections are already set in motion. Whether it's that chance encounter, that unexpected conversation, or the opportunity you weren't even looking for, God is placing the right people on your path. He's aligning the resources and the opportunities that will move you toward the very thing He's called you to do.

I challenge you today: don't let fear or doubt hold you back. Step into the opportunities that come your way, even if they don't make sense at first. Trust that there's a bigger plan unfolding, one that is so intricately designed that all the pieces will fit together in ways you can't yet see. Every connection, every experience, every introduction is part of God's greater plan for your life.

So, take that next step in faith. Reach out to that person. Say yes to the invitation. Walk through the doors that God is opening, and trust that He has already prepared the way. Remember, God doesn't give you a vision without also giving you the people and resources to make it happen. Your connections are waiting—trust God to bring them into your life when the time is right.

Chapter 16: Forgive Yourself

As you move through the journey of transformation, one of the most powerful gifts you can give yourself is grace. This journey isn't always easy. You will come face to face with the experiences of your past—the pain, the mistakes, the things you wish you could go back and change. Some of these things will not have been your fault, and some will. You'll reflect on the moments when you didn't make the best choices, when you acted out of fear, insecurity, or simply didn't know any better. And in those moments of reflection, it's easy to become your own worst critic.

But I want to remind you of this: You are worthy of grace. You are worthy of the same forgiveness, compassion, and understanding that you would offer to a loved one. It's time to extend that same grace to yourself.

There will be times when the weight of your past feels heavy, but holding onto shame or guilt will only hinder your growth. You cannot move forward into the fullness of who you are meant to be if you're constantly dragging the burdens of your past along with you. Yes, take accountability for the choices you made. Acknowledge the mistakes, but don't let them define you. You did the best you could with the knowledge and tools you had at the time. And now that you know better, you can do better.

Grace reminds you that you are not the person you were in the past. You are not bound by those choices. You have the power to grow, to evolve, and to rise above the person you once were. But to do that, you must release yourself from the chains of self-judgment. Forgive yourself for what you didn't know. Forgive yourself for the moments you fell short. You are human, and part of this journey is learning and growing through those missteps.

It's also important to recognize that other people may try to hold you to your past. They may remind you of the mistakes you made, of the times you didn't show up as your best self. But just because they see you through the lens of who you used to be doesn't mean you have to accept that definition. People will often project their own limitations and judgments onto you, but their opinions do not define your worth. You are not obligated to live in the shadow of your past.

Instead, take ownership of your story. Yes, you've made mistakes—but so has everyone. It's part of being human. The key is to own those mistakes, learn from them, and then move forward with grace. Do not let anyone, including yourself, hold you captive to who you used to be. You are a new creation, constantly evolving, growing, and stepping into a higher version of yourself.

Grace allows you to release the past and embrace the present. It allows you to look at yourself with compassion, to see the progress you've made, and to honor the journey you've been on. It's what enables you to continue moving forward, even when the path is challenging.

Inspiring Call to Action

So today, I invite you to give yourself grace. Reflect on your journey—on the moments you stumbled, on the times you didn't know any better—and forgive yourself. You are doing the best you can with what you know now, and that is enough. Don't let the mistakes of the past hold you back. Release them. Move forward. And walk in the fullness of the person you are becoming.

Chapter 17: Re-Create Your Crown

As I reflect on the journey that has brought me to this point, I am filled with deep gratitude for the path I have walked. The challenges, the triumphs, the moments of doubt, and the breakthroughs have all been part of a grand design—one that has shaped me into the person I am today.

My journey has been one of transformation, not just of the mind and body, but of the spirit. It has been a journey of discovering who I truly am, aligning with my purpose, and re-creating the crown that God placed upon my head from the very beginning.

This crown is a symbol of your divine inheritance, your worth, and your identity as a child of God. But over time, through the struggles, challenges, and limiting beliefs, that crown may have become tarnished, forgotten, or even lost.

My journey has been about rediscovering that crown, polishing it, and re-creating it to reflect the fullness of who I am meant to be. And now, I invite you to embark on your own journey to re-create your crown and step into your purpose.

Finding and stepping into your purpose is a critical part of re-creating your crown. So many people struggle with this—wondering what their purpose is, questioning if they're on the right path, and feeling disconnected from their true calling. But your purpose is not something you have to search for outside of yourself. It's not hidden in some far-off place, waiting to be discovered. Your purpose is already within you, woven into the very fabric of your being, and it's revealed as you align with your true self and step into the fullness of who you are.

Re-creating your crown is not just about personal growth—it's about reclaiming your power, your identity, and your purpose. It's about taking the tools and tactics discussed in each episode—meditation, personal development, health, faith, and obedience—and using them to restore and renew the crown that is rightfully yours. But most importantly, it's about recognizing that your crown and your purpose are intertwined. As you polish your crown, you purpose will be revealed. And as you step into your purpose, your crown shines even brighter.

The process of re-creating your crown is both a physical and spiritual journey. It requires you to clear out the clutter of limiting beliefs, to overcome the fears that have held you back, and to embrace the fullness of your potential. It's about recognizing the beauty, strength, and power that have always been within you, and allowing that light to shine brightly for the world to see.

Your purpose is the unique contribution that only you can make in this world. It's the reason you were created, the mission that God has entrusted to you, and the legacy you will leave behind. As you re-create your crown, you will find that each tool you use—whether it's meditation, visualization, or the practice of stillness—brings you closer to your purpose. Each time you choose faith over fear, you step further into the life you were meant to live. Each time you embrace your health and well-being, you strengthen the foundation upon which your purpose stands.

This book has been a reflection of my journey, but it is also an invitation—a call to action for you to embark on your own journey of transformation and crown re-creation. To help you on this path, I've created a workbook designed to guide you through the process of identifying and overcoming your own limiting beliefs, aligning with your purpose, and re-creating the crown that is yours by divine right.

Call to Action

This journey, my journey, was never just about me. It was about each and every one of you who are ready to reclaim the crown that is rightfully yours. Your crown may have been tarnished, lost, or forgotten through the trials, the doubts, the limiting beliefs that life has thrown your way—but it's still there. And now, it's time to re-create it. It's time to step into the fullness of who you are meant to be, to align with your true purpose, and to wear your crown with the strength and grace of a child of God.

The crown on your head is not just a symbol of personal growth—it is a reflection of your divine inheritance, your worth, and your unique power. But here's the truth: no one can re-create your crown for you. No one can step into your purpose except you. And that is your greatest power.

Right now, you stand on the edge of transformation.

RECREATING YOUR CROWN

You've been given the tools—faith, obedience, meditation, health, self-awareness—and now it's time to use them. It's time to clear out the clutter of limiting beliefs, release the fear that's been holding you back, and step into your power. This is your moment to reclaim your crown, to polish it, to let it shine as a beacon of who you truly are. This is your moment to rise.

So, I challenge you: take that first step. Commit to this journey of transformation. Commit to the process of re-creating your crown. Set three specific intentions for the next month that will help you continue to re-create your crown and step into your purpose. You have everything you need inside of you to live the life God has called you to live. Trust that, believe that, and let nothing stand in your way. You are worthy. You are enough. And your purpose is waiting for you.

As we close this chapter, know that this is not the end—it's only the beginning. Season 2 of the Vibrate Higher Podcast is on the horizon, and we're diving deep into the world of energetic frequencies and states of consciousness. It's time to explore how emotions shape your reality, and how you can begin to raise your vibration and vibrate higher. I can't wait to continue this journey with you as we unlock the next level of your transformation.

So, get ready to raise your frequency, get ready to vibrate higher, and get ready to step fully into the person you were always meant to be. Your crown is waiting. It's time to wear it.

Workbook: Re-Create Your Crown (6-Weeks)

Week 1: Identifying and Overcoming Limiting Beliefs

Purpose: To help you identify the beliefs that have been holding you back and guide you through the process of transforming these beliefs and creating new ones.

Day 1-2: Reflective Journaling

• Reflect and journal on your limiting beliefs in each area of your life. (ex. health, appearance, finances, family, love etc.)
• Where did these beliefs originate? What happened in your childhood?

Day 3-4: Challenge Your Beliefs

• Write positive beliefs next to each limiting belief.
• Visualize how your life would change if you embraced these positive beliefs.

Day 5-7: Daily Affirmations

• Create and start using daily affirmations. Start each affirmation with "I AM". (Ex. I am beautiful, I am loving, I am courageous, I am abundant etc).
• Hang your affirmations on your bathroom mirror or somewhere visible, and repeat them daily.

Week 2: Meditation and Stillness Practices

Purpose: To introduce meditation and stillness practices that can hep you connect with your true self and hear God's guidance.

Day 1-2: Creating Your Meditation Space

• Set up a meditation space and choose sounds or objects that help you focus. (Ex. Bob Proctor Meditation on Youtube). Determine what the best time/place will be each day.

Day 3-4: Guided Visualization

• Practice a guided visualization and journal about the experience. Start to think about your goals and what you want to achieve. Start to visualize them and feel the emotions as if it has already happened. What will it feel like? Will you be emotional?

Day 5-6: Vision Board Creation

• Create a vision board that represents your goals and dreams.
• Visualize your future self. Your highest self. Write down what he/she looks like, how does he/she dress, how much money do they make? Are they kind? Are they authentic?
• Spend a few minutes each day visualizing a specific goal as if it has already been achieved. Journal about your experiences.

Day 7: Daily Stillness Practice

• Commit to 5-10 minutes of daily stillness and journal any changes.
• Incorporate meditation or stillness into your morning routine and reflect on any improvements in your day.

Week 3: Overcoming Fear and Embracing Failure

Purpose: To empower you to face your fears, reframe failure, and take bold action towards your goals.

Day 1-2: Fear Inventory

- List and analyze your top fears. Reflect on the worst and best outcomes if those fears were faced.

Day 3-5: Reframing Failure

- Reflect on a past failure, write about the lessons learned, and apply them to your current goals.

Day 6-7: Taking Bold Action

- Choose one action step you've been avoiding due to fear and commit to taking it. Journal about the experience.

Week 4: Health and Wellness

Purpose: To guide you in making small but impactful changes to your diet, exercise routine, and self-care practices that support your physical, mental, and spiritual well-being.

Day 1-2: Dietary Reflection

- Reflect on your current diet and choose one small change to eat cleaner. Try adding something healthy to your diet versus taking away.

Day 3-4: Mindful Eating Exercise

- Practice mindful eating and journal about how it affects your relationship with food.

Day 5-7: Exercise Routine

- Incorporate regular physical activity into your week. At least 30 min per day. Track its impact on your overall health and mental clarity.

Week 5: Faith and Obedience

Purpose: To deepen faith and help you practice obedience to God's call, aligning your actions with His will.

Day 1-3: Faith Reflection

- Reflect on your current relationship with faith and how it has guided you. Do you tend to worry often? Do you tend to toss and turn at night due to anxiety?

Day 4-6: Obedience in Action

- Identify an area where you feel called to act and take a step-in obedience.

Day 7: Surrender Exercise

- Surrender a goal to God in prayer or meditation and reflect on the experience.

Week 6: Final Reflection and Commitments

Purpose: To help you reflect on your journey through the workbook and set intentions for continued growth.

Day 1-2: Looking Back

- Reflect on the changes made throughout the workbook and write about the lessons learned.

Day 3-4: Future Commitments

- Set three specific intentions for the next month that will help you continue to re-create your crown and step into your purpose.

Day 5-7: Visualization and Goal Setting

- Visualize your life with these intentions fully realized and set actionable goals for the next steps in your journey.

Acknowledgements

First and foremost, I want to thank God for guiding me through every step of this journey. Without His love, grace, and guidance, none of this would have been possible. I am forever grateful for the strength and wisdom He has given me to overcome the challenges I've faced and to re-create my crown.

To my mother, thank you for your unwavering strength, tenacity, support, and love. I know that life has not always been easy, but you faced every challenge with courage and determination. You did the best you could with what you had, and I am forever grateful for the sacrifices you made for us. Your resilience has been a constant source of inspiration to me, and I admire the way you never gave up, even in the face of adversity. Our journey together has made our bond stronger, and I am so thankful for the wonderful relationship we have today. Your support means the world to me, and I am blessed to have you as my #1 supporter. This book is as much a testament to your strength as it is to my own. Thank you for believing in me, for standing by me, and for showing me the true meaning of love and perseverance.

To my sister, I want you to know how much I love and appreciate you. When you left for the Marines, it was a pivotal time in my life, and though I felt alone, I never resented you for it. You were on your own journey, battling your own challenges, and I understand that now more than ever. You tried to be there for me in the ways you could, and I've always felt your love. I want you to know that I've always admired your strength and resilience, and I will forever love you. Thank you for everything and know that I carry your support with me always.

To my mentors, thank you for your guidance and wisdom. You have helped me see the world in new ways and have given me the tools to grow and evolve into the person I am today.

About the Author: De'iona Monay

De'iona Monay is a passionate advocate for personal growth, empowerment, and transformation. Having overcome her own struggles with limiting beliefs, she is dedicated to helping others find their voice, reclaim their power, and live a life of purpose and fulfillment. Through her work as an inspirational speaker, youth mentor, and author, she shares her story and the lessons she has learned to inspire others to embark on their own journeys of healing and self-discovery.

Contact the Author:

email: deionamonay@gmail.com
website: https://www.deionamonay.com
Instagram: @deionamonay

RECREATING YOUR CROWN

Milton Keynes UK
Ingram Content Group UK Ltd.
UKHW051852281024
450367UK00019B/263